A Note to Parents and Teachers

DK READERS is a compelling reading programme for

001915

Eton Academy
Library
This book is due for return on or before the last date shown below.

0 8 OCT 2021

ABERDEENSHIRE
LIBRARIES

WITHDRAWN
FROM LIBRARY

Wright Brothers
J629.
13
1406231

629.13

AB
D0270609

001915/428.6

LONDON, NEW YORK, DELHI,
MUNICH AND MELBOURNE

Project Editor Caroline Bingham
Art Editor Helen Chapman
Series Editor Deborah Lock
Senior Art Editor Cheryl Telfer
DTP designer Almudena Díaz
Production Shivani Pandey
Picture Researcher Bridget Tily
Illustrator Peter Dennis
Jacket Designer Dean Price
Indexer Lynn Bresler

Curatorial review Peter Jakab
National Air and Space Museum
©2002 Smithsonian Institution

Reading Consultant
Cliff Moon M.Ed.

Published in Great Britian by
Dorling Kindersley Limited
80, The Strand, London WC2R ORL
2 4 6 8 10 9 7 5 3 1

Copyright © 2003 Dorling Kindersley Limited, London

All rights reserved. No part of this publication may be reproduced, stored
in a retrieval system, or transmitted in any form or by any means,
electronic, mechanical, photocopying, recording, or otherwise, without
the prior written permission of the copyright owner.

A CIP record for this book is available
from the British Library

ISBN 0-7513-6795-8

Color reproduction by Colourscan, Singapore
Printed and bound in China by L Rex Printing Co., Ltd.

The publisher would like to thank the following for their kind permission
to reproduce their photographs:
a=above; c=centre; b=below; l=left; r=right t=top;

Mike Booher: 38c; Corbis: 15tr, 42tl; Bettmann 20tl; Underwood and
Underwood 3c; The Flight Collection: 46b; Getty Images: 7tr, 12tl, 14tl,
14bl; Hayward Gallery Library: Tetra Associates. Photo: Ian Hessenberg
4c; Stephen Oliver: 11tr; Quadrant Picture Library: Jeremy Hoare 37tr;
Science & Society Picture Library: 5tr, 5br, 17c, 31br, 39tr; National
Museum of Photography, Film & TV 30bl; Science Photo Library: 25tr;
CNRI 12bl; Tektoff-Merieux CNRI 18tl; Courtesy of the Wright Brothers
Aeroplane Company: 13tr, 22tl; Special Collections and Archives, Wright
State University: 6tl, 6bl, 9tr, 9br, 16bl, 18bl, 24b, 27c, 28tl, 28b, 29tr,
31tr, 32c, 34tl, 34bl, 35tr, 35br, 36c, 39br, 40tl, 40b, 41r, 42b, 43tr, 44tl,
44b, 46l. Jacket images : Corbis Bettmann front t, back tr; Popperfoto
front b, back tl.

All other images © Dorling Kindersley.
For further imformation see: www.dkimages.com

see our complete catalogue at
www.dk.com

Contents

PROFICIENT
4
READERS

FIRST FLIGHT

THE STORY OF
THE WRIGHT BROTHERS

Written by Caryn Jenner

A Dorling Kindersley Book

Icarus
In the ancient myth, the Sun melted Icarus's wings and he fell into the sea. Some people saw this as a warning that humans were not meant to fly.

Flying machines

Today, air travel is commonplace, thanks to the amazing invention of Wilbur and Orville Wright. But in past centuries, people could only imagine what it would be like to fly.

An ancient Greek myth tells the story of Daedalus and Icarus, who made wings from feathers and wax.

J629.13
1406231

Leonardo da Vinci
This model of an ornithopter is based on sketches by the Italian artist and scientist, Leonardo da Vinci. He thought that the flapping wings of a bird held the key to human flight.

Much later, others, such as Leonardo da Vinci, tried to invent flying machines. In the 15th century, da Vinci designed a machine with enormous flapping wings, and had ideas for a helicopter and a parachute. However, his machines would not have been able to fly.

In 1783, the Montgolfier brothers from France invented the hot-air balloon. Because the hot air in a balloon is lighter than the cold air around it, the balloon rises. The hot-air balloon is a "lighter-than-air" flying machine.

In the first half of the 1800s, Sir George Cayley became a true pioneer in the science of flight. He designed the first glider. At the end of the century, Otto Lilienthal flew his own gliders, although his flights were unsteady and brief. It was up to Wilbur and Orville Wright to make the dream of flight a reality.

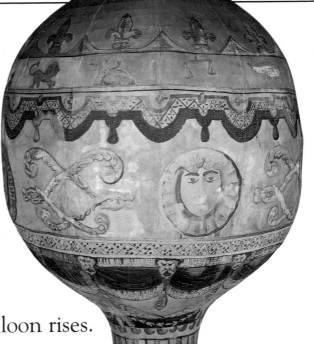

Montgolfier balloon
The hot-air balloon allowed people to look down from the sky for the first time.

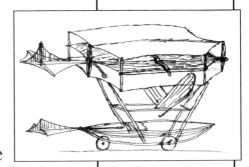

Cayley's glider

Wilbur Wright
Wilbur was born on August 16, 1867. He was hard-working and enjoyed sports.

Orville Wright
Orville was born on August 19, 1871. As a child, he was often very mischievous. These photos were taken in 1878.

The toy helicopter

DATE
1878

Wilbur and Orville Wright couldn't wait to see the surprise their father had brought home for them.

"Here it is, boys!"

Their father tossed a small toy into the air. Instead of falling, the toy rose up towards the ceiling. Wilbur and Orville watched in amazement.

"It flies!" exclaimed Orville.

"But how does it fly?" Wilbur wondered.

The two brothers studied the toy helicopter and discovered that it was powered by twisting an elastic band. As they let the helicopter go, the elastic band unwound, causing the propeller to spin quickly and the helicopter to fly in the air. As the propeller slowed down, the helicopter wobbled, then fell to the ground.

"Let's make our own helicopters, Orville," Wilbur suggested.

So the boys experimented with their own versions of the toy helicopter. They found that the bigger the helicopter was, the quicker it fell to the ground.

Later, while inventing the first aeroplane, the Wright brothers would remember the toy helicopters that were their first flying machines.

Elastic band
When you stretch or twist an elastic band, it uses force in order to spring back to its usual size. The brothers' helicopter used a twisted elastic band at its centre. The boys called their toy helicopters "bats".

Woodcuts
To make a woodcut, Orville carved a picture into a block of wood. Then he dipped the wood into some ink and printed the picture onto a piece of paper.

As they grew older, the Wright brothers could often be found making things and experimenting.

Wilbur invented a machine to fold the newspapers that his father sent around the United States.

Orville loved to make and fly kites. He even made kites to sell to his friends. He was also interested in printing with woodcuts.

The boys' parents, Milton and Susan Wright, encouraged their curiosity. They wanted their children to learn as much as they could, and the house was filled with books.

Unlike most women in the 1800s, Susan had gone to college. Milton was a minister who travelled around the country. He also edited a religious newspaper.

Wilbur and Orville had two older brothers and a younger sister, but the two younger boys were especially close. Wilbur once said, "From the time we were little children, my brother Orville and myself lived together, worked together and, in fact, thought together."

Throughout their lives, the brothers worked as a team.

Susan Wright
The boys' mother was handy with tools and often built things for the children.

Milton Wright
Their father wrote many letters home telling his family about the places he visited.

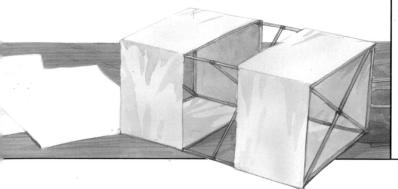

Dayton, Ohio
During the late 1800s, Dayton became a prosperous, industrial city, thanks mainly to the arrival of the railway.

USA
Dayton •

Apprentice
Orville was an apprentice for a local printer. An apprentice gained hands-on practice in a business, but didn't earn a regular salary. Today, an apprentice is sometimes called a "trainee".

Brothers in business

DATE
1884

The Wright family moved back to Dayton, Ohio, USA, where they had once lived.

Orville soon became friends with a boy named Ed Sines, who ran a small printing press. The two friends went into partnership and started printing signs and advertising leaflets for local businesses.

During his summer holidays from school, Orville became an apprentice to a local printer. With Wilbur's help, he and Ed built a bigger printing press using materials from a scrapyard.

One day, the town grocer gave Orville and Ed some popcorn as payment for printing a sign.

"Popcorn won't buy more type for the printing press," Orville grumbled. "We need money for that."

Ed shrugged. "I'll have your popcorn if you don't want it, Orville," he said.

Orville and Ed made a deal. Ed sold his share of the printing business to Orville in exchange for Orville's popcorn. Both boys were delighted with the deal.

Orville's printing business grew, and he moved it to a shop in the centre of Dayton.

Printing press
Orville and Ed set type onto the flat surface and inked it, then placed the paper on top. A weight was used to transfer ink from the type to paper.

Type
In the early 1900s, type came in metal blocks. Each letter had to be set individually.

False teeth
In the 1880s, false teeth were made from baked minerals and fixed into a rubber base.

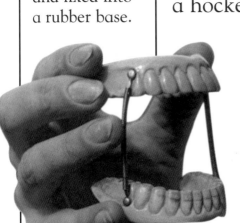

Tuberculosis
Tuberculosis (TB) is caused by bacteria. It can now be cured but it used to kill a lot of people.

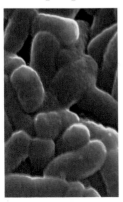

Meanwhile, Wilbur was looking forward to going to college. He was also keen on playing sports. During a hockey game, a player hit him in the face with a hockey stick. Several of Wilbur's teeth were knocked out and he had to have false ones.

The injuries healed, but Wilbur lost his confidence and became very quiet. He decided not to go to college after all.

At the same time, Susan Wright was suffering from a lung disease called tuberculosis. Wilbur nursed his mother, but she died in 1889. The entire family mourned, but Wilbur had grown particularly close to his mother, and he felt very upset.

Orville thought that Wilbur needed something to keep him busy. He asked his brother to help him start a newspaper called the *West Side News*. Wilbur enjoyed writing for this and other newspapers that the brothers published. He had always followed current affairs, but now he paid special attention. He wrote articles in support of women's right to vote and other main issues.

Newspapers
The slogan for the Wright brothers' newspapers was: "All the news of the world that most people care to read, and in such a shape the people will have time to read it".

The bicycle boom

DATE
1892

The Wright brothers found a new interest when Orville bought a safety bicycle. It was called a safety bicycle because the front and back wheels were the same size, so it was safer to ride than the old-style "penny-farthing" bicycles.

"I feel like I'm flying!" Orville called to Wilbur, as he zoomed past on his new bike. Soon, Wilbur bought a safety bike, too. In fact, the invention of the safety bicycle started a craze for cycling. Like many bicycle enthusiasts of the time, the Wright brothers joined a cycling club.

They went for bicycle rides in the countryside with the club, and Orville even won some races.

The Wright brothers were also skilled at repairing bicycles. Soon, cycling enthusiasts in Dayton were bringing their bikes to Wilbur and Orville to be fixed. The brothers saw a new business opportunity. They made Ed Sines manager of the print shop and opened a bicycle repair shop across the street.

SPRINGFIELD BICYCLE CLUB.

BICYCLE CAMP-EXHIBITION & TOURNAMENT.
SPRINGFIELD, MASS. U.S.A. SEPT. 18.19.20. 1883.

Bicycle clubs
Cycling was also called "wheeling". It was a fun method of travel for both men and women, and it was also a popular social activity.

The Wright brothers' cycle shop

Van Cleve
The Van Cleve bicycle was named after an Ohio pioneer who was related to the Wright family.

The Wright Cycle Company became a thriving business. As well as repairing bicycles, Wilbur and Orville began making bikes to sell. They ordered parts from bicycle factories, then fitted them together to their own designs, making improvements. They called their special models the St. Clair and the Van Cleve.

By 1896, there was another new form of travel on the streets of Dayton. The brothers' friend, Cord Ruse, built the first motor car in town.

"Why fiddle with bicycles when you can have a horseless carriage?" called Cord, as his car spluttered and clanked outside the cycle shop. "I just fill it with petrol and off it goes."

Orville laughed. "Just don't lose any of those nuts and bolts I hear rattling around."

"You should attach a big bed sheet under the engine to catch those loose parts, Cord," added Wilbur.

Cars did not have the same attraction for the Wright brothers as bicycles did and neither brother believed that cars would catch the public's imagination. But there was another form of travel that would soon begin to fascinate them – flying machines.

The horseless carriage
A "horseless carriage" was another name for a car. Early cars were noisy and dusty, and often unreliable.

Petrol
Car engines burn petrol for fuel. The Wright brothers also used petrol to fuel the engines of their aeroplanes.

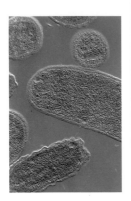

Typhoid
Typhoid bacteria cause high fever. Orville's fever was so high that he was sometimes delirious.

Otto Lilienthal
Otto Lilienthal made over 2,000 glider flights but he had limited control of the glider.

Aiming for the sky

DATE
1896

Orville became very sick with typhoid. Wilbur and the rest of the family were worried, but Orville slowly began to get better. During this time, Wilbur read about the death of Otto Lilienthal, a German glider pilot who died when his glider crashed. The brothers admired Lilienthal's accomplishments in his glider. Once again, their thoughts turned towards the challenges of flight.

They decided that there were three main requirements for a practical flying machine. First, the pilot had to be in control of the aircraft. Second, the design of the wings had to provide lift for the aircraft. Third, a practical aircraft had to be powered by an engine so that the aircraft could stay up for a long time.

Otto Lilienthal takes to the skies in his glider.

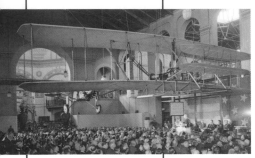

For the next few years, Wilbur and Orville read as much as they could about flying in books and scientific magazines. They sent for more information from the Smithsonian Institution in Washington, D.C., USA.

Smithsonian Institution
The Smithsonian Institution promotes research in many different subjects. Today, you can visit the Smithsonian museums in Washington, D.C., USA.

The brothers learned all about the different types of flying machines that had already been tried. They learned about birds and observed them flying. Balance seemed to be the key to flying, just as in riding a bicycle.

Wilbur and Orville decided to experiment with a biplane, and focus on a way to control the aircraft before they added an engine.

"Birds only have to twist their wings slightly in order to control their flight," said Orville.

"We might be able to control our aircraft if we can find a way to twist the wings," said Wilbur. "But how?"

Biplane
A biplane is an aircraft that has two wings, one on top of the other. The Frenchman Louis Blériot was the first to experiment with a monoplane – a one-wing aircraft.

Bird flight
The flight of birds is very complicated. The flapping of the wings, and the opening and closing of the feathers to push against the air or let the air slip through helps the bird to lift, swoop and soar.

Box twisting
Wilbur imagined that the box was twisting like the parallel wings of a biplane.

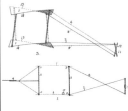

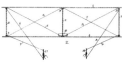

Kite sketch
Wilbur's sketch shows how the wings twist slightly, like the wings of a bird.

DATE
1899

One summer day, Wilbur was working in the bicycle shop. As he absentmindedly twisted the ends of a long, thin box, he had an idea.

The brothers made a large biplane kite. Ropes ran from the front corners of the wings to two sticks that were used to control the kite from the ground. When the sticks were tugged, the corners of the wings twisted slightly, changing the direction of the kite. This twisting mechanism became known as wing-warping.

Wilbur tested the kite while Orville was camping with friends.

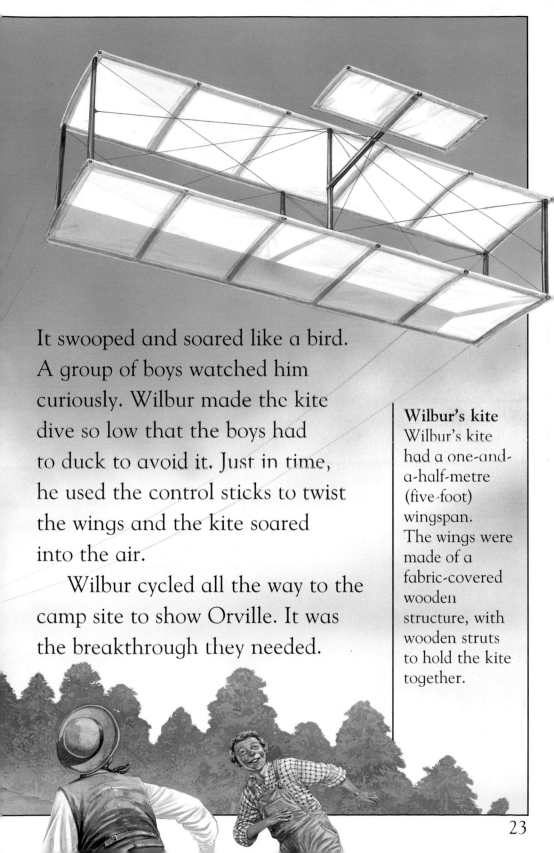

It swooped and soared like a bird. A group of boys watched him curiously. Wilbur made the kite dive so low that the boys had to duck to avoid it. Just in time, he used the control sticks to twist the wings and the kite soared into the air.

Wilbur cycled all the way to the camp site to show Orville. It was the breakthrough they needed.

Wilbur's kite
Wilbur's kite had a one-and-a-half-metre (five-foot) wingspan. The wings were made of a fabric-covered wooden structure, with wooden struts to hold the kite together.

Elevator
One reason for placing the elevator at the front was the protection it would provide in case of a crash.

Kitty Hawk
Along with its advantages, Kitty Hawk also had disadvantages, such as sandstorms caused by the strong winds.

Flying experiments

DATE
1900

The brothers spent about a year making their first glider. It was based on their kite, but much bigger, with wings that were 5 metres (17 feet) long from tip to tip. They added a flat section at the front of the lower wing, called an elevator. The pilot would lie down on the wings.

The Wright brothers would need a windy place to test their glider.

After studying information from the United States Weather Bureau, they decided on Kitty Hawk, an isolated fishing village on the coast of North Carolina.

Kitty Hawk was an excellent testing site in many ways. Along with steady winds, there were tall sand dunes to help launch the glider, few buildings or trees to crash into, and open stretches of sand to cushion any falls. There were also very few people, so the Wright brothers could conduct their experiments without publicity.

US Weather Bureau
The Weather Bureau keeps records of weather patterns around the USA. With the development of satellites, they can also predict weather.

Packing
Wilbur and Orville had built the glider in Dayton, then taken it apart and packed the pieces into crates that Wilbur took with him.

Wilbur left for Kitty Hawk in early September while Orville sorted things out at the bicycle shop. Wilbur took with him most of the parts for the glider and the tools needed to assemble it. He also took a large tent.

Wilbur's journey from Dayton to Kitty Hawk began with a 24-hour train ride. Then he took a ferry, and then another train. Finally, he hired a fisherman to take him the rest of the way in his boat.

USA

Dayton

Kitty Hawk

Train
As the Wright brothers were beginning to experiment with flight, there were big advances in train systems. Electric trains were beginning to make an appearance.

A few hours after setting sail, the boat got caught in a severe storm. In the dark of night, huge waves bounced the tiny boat. Fierce winds ripped the sails. The fisherman had to anchor the boat in a sheltered cove for the night. Wilbur slept on the hard deck. The storm passed and Wilbur arrived in Kitty Hawk late the following night.

The camp site
Wilbur stayed with postmaster Bill Tate and his family until Orville arrived. Then a large tent became the brothers' home and workshop.

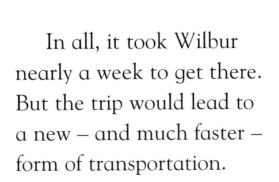
Wilbur outside the tent.

In all, it took Wilbur nearly a week to get there. But the trip would lead to a new – and much faster – form of transportation.

Tent life
On several occasions, the wind was so strong that the tent nearly blew away.

Tom Tate
Tom Tate was
the nephew of
Kitty Hawk's
postmaster.
Orville said
that Tom could
"tell more big
yarns than any
kid of his size
I ever saw".

The brothers began by flying the glider like a kite. The glider was large and the controls took practice to master. Within three days, it crashed! Although disappointed, the brothers soon repaired it.

Sometimes a local boy named Tom Tate rode the glider while the brothers controlled it from the ground. Sometimes Wilbur flew the glider himself.

The brothers realised that in order to fly better, the glider needed more upward movement, or lift.

The following summer, in 1901, they returned to Kitty Hawk with a new glider. Flight pioneer Octave Chanute observed their experiments and he was impressed.

But Wilbur and Orville were far from satisfied. The lift was still not good enough and now there were problems with the controls.

Octave Chanute
Octave Chanute spent many years experimenting with flight before meeting the Wright brothers.

Lift
The air current beneath the wings gives an aircraft its lift.

Photography
Photography was a popular hobby of the time. Orville used a shed as a darkroom to develop photographs.

Camera
Early cameras took negatives of a picture on a metal plate instead of film.

Back in Dayton, Orville developed the latest photographs from Kitty Hawk. The pictures had recorded the glider experiments. When they analysed data from their gliding experiments, they didn't make sense when compared to established data from Lilienthal and other flight pioneers.

"We've been relying on data collected by other people," said Orville, "but what if they're wrong?"

"We'll have to test all of the data ourselves," Wilbur replied.

Testing the data would prove a long task. They built a small wind tunnel. A fan at one end provided the wind. Inside, the brothers placed miniature wings, or airfoils, mounted to test instruments so they could measure the lift and drag (the wings lifting or slowing down in the airflow). This was done to find the wing's ideal curve, or camber, for flight. Although time-consuming, they both realised that the research was necessary.

Meanwhile, the Wrights were introduced to other experimenters. Octave Chanute had invited Wilbur to give an important lecture about human flight. For the occasion, Wilbur borrowed clothes from Orville's more stylish wardrobe. The speech was a great success.

Wind tunnel
With the wind tunnel, the Wright brothers simulated flying conditions for their tests.

Always in style
Orville was known for his fashionable clothes.
He always liked to look smart, even when the work was dirty.

Wing length
The brothers thought that the longer, narrower wings would improve lift.

DATE
1902

Using their new data, the Wright brothers designed a glider with longer, narrower wings and a different camber, or curve. They also redesigned the shape of the elevator at the front of the lower wing and added a fixed tail.

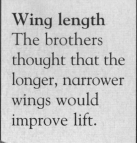

Rudder
A movable rudder turns the aircraft by directing the airflow on either side.

With high hopes, they went to Kitty Hawk. They immediately noticed the improved lift, but the fixed tail made control harder.

"Let's make the tail into a movable rudder to help with steering," suggested Orville.

Wilbur agreed. "We'll connect the rudder controls and the wing-warping controls so the pilot can work them together."

The brothers made the necessary changes and the plan worked. Wing-warping enabled the glider to roll by raising one wing and dipping the other. The elevator controlled pitch, moving the nose of the glider up or down. The movable rudder controlled yaw, turning the nose left or right. These three forms of control are still used in aircraft today.

Wilbur and Orville flew the improved glider again and again – sometimes 100 flights in one day at distances of more than 182 metres (600 feet)! They had mastered the control and the lift of the aircraft. Now they turned their attention to adding power.

Roll
Roll allows the aircraft to bank, so that one wing is up, while the other is down.

Pitch
Pitch moves the nose up or down. For take off, the pitch needs to be up so the aircraft will rise.

Yaw
Yaw turns the aircraft left or right, pointing it in the direction of the flight path.

Engine

The Wright brothers could not find a manufacturer to make a suitable engine, so they made one specially for the Flyer.

Aerodrome

Samuel Langley's pilot survived two crashes in his Aerodrome. The press made fun of Langley's attempts to fly, and Wilbur was wary of their reaction to his own trials.

The Wright Flyer

DATE 1903

With the help of Charlie Taylor, the mechanic at the bicycle shop, Wilbur and Orville built a small, light-weight engine. The Wright Flyer was the largest aircraft the Wrights had ever built. Orville called it a "whopper flying machine".

But at Kitty Hawk, parts kept breaking. Orville had to bring the propeller shafts, which held the propellers, back to Dayton for repair.

On the train back, he read newspaper reports about Samuel Langley's flying machine, which had crashed into a river near Washington, D.C., USA.

On December 14, the Wright brothers were finally ready to attempt a flight.

The Kitty Hawk lifesaving crew arrived to help. The brothers flipped a coin to see who would be the pilot. Wilbur won.

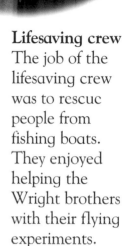

The engine rumbled. Orville ran alongside to balance the wings, then the aeroplane flew off the launching rail and into the sky. The plane rose up sharply. Suddenly, it slowed, stalled, and the Wright Flyer sank into the sand.

The brothers were disappointed, but the flight had proved that the aeroplane could take off under the power of its own engine.

Lifesaving crew
The job of the lifesaving crew was to rescue people from fishing boats. They enjoyed helping the Wright brothers with their flying experiments.

Winter weather
When the Wright brothers awoke on the morning of December 17, 1903, and saw the bad weather, they discussed their options. They decided that despite the weather, they didn't want to wait any longer. They would try to fly again.

Bad weather meant the brothers had to wait to try again.

On December 17, the wind was still gusting, but Wilbur and Orville were anxious to be home for Christmas, so they decided to have another attempt.

It was Orville's turn to fly. They set up the camera and asked John Daniels, a member of the lifesaving crew, to take a picture as

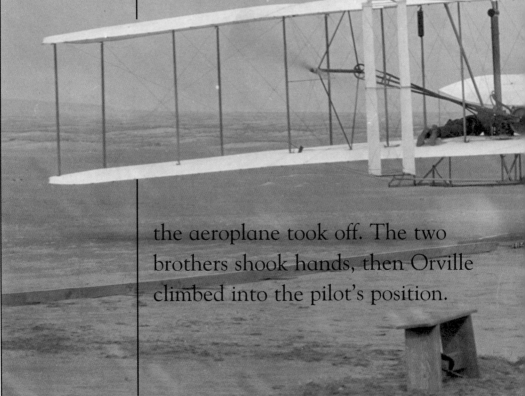

the aeroplane took off. The two brothers shook hands, then Orville climbed into the pilot's position.

Everyone was solemn on what they hoped would be an historic day.

"Don't look so serious," Wilbur urged. "Laugh and cheer and shout!"

The crew called encouragement as Orville took off. Quickly, Daniels snapped the photograph as proof of the flight. The Flyer climbed and dived, up and down, several times, as Orville tried to steady the nose of the aeroplane.

How far was the first flight? The first controlled, powered flight was about 37 metres (120 feet). That is shorter than the main passenger cabin of a modern 747 jumbo jet.

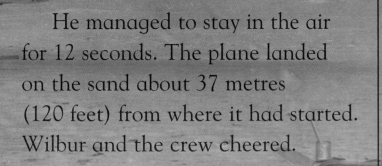

He managed to stay in the air for 12 seconds. The plane landed on the sand about 37 metres (120 feet) from where it had started. Wilbur and the crew cheered.

National memorial
An 18-metre (60-foot) granite monument was erected in 1932 to mark the site of the Wright brothers' flights on December 17, 1903.

Four flight markers
The distances flown on the four flights are marked at the site of the Wright brothers' National memorial.

The Wright brothers were delighted. Despite the strong wind, they took turns flying for a total of four flights.

During the fourth flight, the Flyer pitched up and down as Wilbur struggled to control the elevator – too far forwards and the nose dived, too far back and it climbed too quickly. Finally it sank onto the sand. The flight had covered 260 metres (852 feet) and lasted 59 seconds.

As Wilbur, Orville and the lifesaving crew looked at the Flyer, a gust of wind rolled it over on the sand. Daniels tried to stop it, but when the Flyer finally came to rest, it had been reduced to a heap of broken wood and torn cloth. But the brothers had achieved their aim.

Johnny Moore, the youngest member of the lifesaving crew, was so excited, he raced to the village shouting, "They did it!"

Wilbur and Orville sat down to a quiet lunch. Then they sent a telegram home to their father and sister, telling them of the day's success, and adding that they would be home for Christmas.

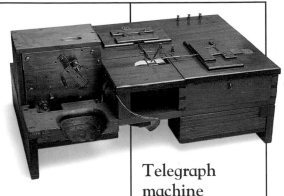

Telegraph machine
A telegram was the quickest way to send a message over long distances. The telegraph machine sent electrical signals over wires.

Form No. 168.

THE WESTERN UNION TELEGRAPH COMPANY.

INCORPORATED

23,000 OFFICES IN AMERICA. CABLE SERVICE TO ALL THE WORLD.

This Company TRANSMITS and DELIVERS messages only o.. conditions limiting its liability, which have been assented to by the sender of the following message. Errors can be guarded against only by repeating a message back to the sending station for comparison, and the Company will not hold itself liable for errors or delays in transmission or delivery of Unrepeated Messages, beyond the amount of tolls paid thereon, nor in any case where the claim is not presented in writing within sixty days after the message is filed with the Company for transmission. and is delivered by request of the sender, under the conditions named above.
This is an UNREPEATED MESSAGE, and is delivered by request of the sender, under the conditions named above.

ROBERT C. CLOWRY, President and General Manager.

170

RECEIVED at

176 C KA GS 33 Paid.   Via Norfolk Va

Kitty Hawk N C Dec 17

Bishop M Wright

            7 Hawthorne St

Success four flights thursday morning all against twenty one mile wind started from Level with engine power alone average speed through air thirty one miles longest 57 seconds inform Press

                                    Orevelle Wright   525P

home ~~Phhth~~ Christmas .

Orville's telegram incorrectly recorded the longest flight as lasting 57 seconds, and misspelt his name.

Catapult launcher
The catapult launcher had a pulley hanging from a tower. One end of the pulley held a weight. The other end was attached to a dolly holding the Flyer. When the weight dropped, the dolly zoomed forwards, giving the Flyer enough speed for take off.

Wilbur and Orville continued their experiments at a field near Dayton called Huffman Prairie. They built the Flyer II, a close copy of the original Flyer. In May, they invited reporters to watch a test flight. But the Flyer II hardly got off the ground. It needed more power to make up for the lack of wind in Dayton.

The brothers built a catapult launcher to boost speed during take off. They began to fly longer distances and turn in the air. In September, Orville flew the first complete circle around Huffman Prairie.

But the Flyer II continued to have control problems.

Then they added weight to the front of the plane to improve control further. The Flyer III worked.

On October 5, 1905, a small crowd watched as Wilbur flew around and around Huffman Prairie for a total of 39 kilometres (24 miles). He landed after 39 minutes only because the engine had run out of fuel. It was by far the longest flight in history. The Wright brothers were now confident that they had invented a practical powered aircraft and in 1906 they received a patent for it.

Longest flight
Wilbur's flight on October 5, 1905, was longer than all of the brothers' flights in 1903 and 1904 put together.

Legal patent
A patent gives legal ownership of an invention. No one can use the idea without permission from the inventors.

Aeroplane seats
Early aeroplane seats were open to the weather and the pilots had to dress in warm clothes.

Passengers
The first real aeroplane passenger was Charlie Furnas, the Wrights' mechanic.

Flying far

Now Wilbur and Orville wanted to go into business selling their aeroplanes. But they had trouble persuading people that their aeroplane was a practical flying machine. At last, the United States Army and a company in France both showed interest. At the Army's request, the brothers added space for a passenger and included seats for both the pilot and the passenger. They built two aeroplanes.

The crash that killed Lt. Thomas Selfridge.

In 1908, Wilbur sailed to France to demonstrate one of the planes, while Orville demonstrated the other near Washington, D.C. Both displays started quietly. Then they both began staying in the air longer and longer, amazing the growing crowds below. News of the "birdmen" spread.

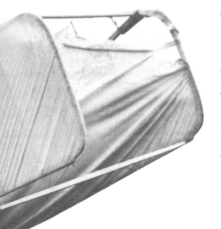

Newspapers pictured the brothers in competition. Wilbur and Orville took it all in fun.

"Your dandy flights make me look like a dud!" Wilbur joked in a letter from France.

Sadly, one of Orville's flights in September ended in tragedy with the death of his passenger, Lieutenant Thomas Selfridge.

Birdman
This cartoon of Wilbur as a birdman was published in a French newspaper. His flights inspired many French aviators, who later broke Wilbur's own records.

Orville's crash
Lt. Thomas Selfridge was the first person to be killed in an aeroplane. The brothers were very upset. When Orville found that a broken propeller blade caused the crash, they reinforced all of the blades to make flying as safe as possible.

A flight for a king?
The King of England (above right) wanted to go on a flight with Wilbur but his royal advisors wouldn't let him.

DATE 1909

Back in the United States, the Wright brothers were national heroes. They even received an award at the White House from President Taft, and they met the King of England, Edward VII. In Dayton, there was a carnival and fireworks in their honour. Wilbur and Orville were embarrassed by the attention but the rest of their family was full of pride.

The brothers set up the Wright Company to manufacture and sell aeroplanes. They also trained pilots to perform at exhibitions.

In October, nearly one million people gazed up at the sky in amazement as Wilbur flew over New York during the Hudson-Fulton celebrations. They cheered, tooting the horns of boats and cars. With so many witnesses to Wilbur's flight, many more people began to believe that humans could fly.

In 1910, the Wright brothers had one of their greatest thrills when Orville took their father for his first flight. Milton Wright was 81 years old.

"Higher, Orville!" he called. "Higher!"

Hudson-Fulton Celebration
This two-week-long celebration honoured explorer Henry Hudson and inventor Robert Fulton – famous pioneers of the past. Wilbur's flight celebrated the future.

Flips and Flops

Flips and Flops had two clowns that spun around a trapeze. One of the older Wright brothers opened a toy factory to manufacture it for sale to the public.

Flyer III

Biplane

In 1912, Wilbur died of typhoid, the same disease that had nearly killed Orville so many years before.

Orville sold his share of the Wright Company a few years later. Sometimes, he still invented small things, such as a toy called Flips and Flops for his nieces and nephews. In 1948, he died quietly in Dayton.

Airliner

Airliner

Airliners developed to carry people from place to place, on holiday or on business. By the 1950s, airliners were carrying about 100 passengers at a time.

With the invention of the aeroplane, Wilbur and Orville Wright made the dream of flight a reality. Flying makes travel easier and quicker, and as a result we know more about different people and places in all corners of the globe.

Military operations have altered dramatically through the development of aircraft.

The invention of the aeroplane has also led to technology that enables us to explore space, and that has led to communication satellites that allow telephones and computers to transmit signals around the world.

Concorde
This supersonic plane flies faster than sound travels through the air. It is the fastest passenger plane and takes only four hours to fly from London to New York.

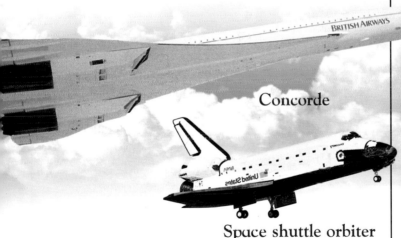

Concorde

Space shuttle orbiter

Space shuttle
The space shuttle's orbiter blasts off into space on the back of a throwaway fuel tank and two solid fuel rockets. It glides back to Earth to land on a runway. The orbiter is designed to fly on about 100 missions.

When the young Wright brothers watched their toy helicopter fly into the air, they didn't know that in years to come they would invent their own flying machine that would change the world.

Glossary

Airflow
The movement of air in a certain direction.

Airfoil
A part of an aircraft, such as a wing, with curved surfaces that help to provide lift during flight.

Biplane
An aircraft with two wings, one above the other.

Camber
A curved surface, as in the curve of a wing.

Data
Information, such as measurements, used in research.

Drag
The air current that pushes back against an aircraft.

Elevator
A flat surface that tilts to control the up and down movement of an aircraft's nose.

Engine
A mechanical device that provides power.

Fuel
A material, such as petrol, that is burned for power.

Glider
An aircraft with wings but no power. A glider must use natural airflow to stay airborne.

Helicopter
An aircraft with propellers on top that give it lift.

Hot-air balloon
A balloon that rises because the hot air inside it is lighter than the cold air around it. A hot-air balloon is a "lighter than air" flying machine.

Lift
The upward force of the airflow that enables an aircraft to take off and to stay in the air.

Pioneer
A person, such as an inventor or explorer, who does something that hasn't been done before.

Pitch
The up and down movement of an aircraft's nose.

Propeller
Blades that push the air around, propelling an aircraft forward.

Roll
Tilting one wing of the aircraft up and the other down.

Thrust
A force that moves an aircraft forwards.

Wing-warping
A control mechanism on an aircraft in which the wings twist slightly, changing the airflow.

Yaw
The movement of the aircraft to the left or right.